Contents

1 The Largest Land
   Animal   4

2 The Trunk   8

3 The Tusks   14

4 New Words   22

5 To Find Out More   23

6 Index   24

7 About the Author   24

The **African elephant** is the largest animal that lives on land.

Animals of the World

African Elephant

By Edana Eckart

Welcome
Books™

Children's Press®
A Division of Scholastic Inc.
New York / Toronto / London / Auckland / Sydney
Mexico City / New Delhi / Hong Kong
Danbury, Connecticut

Photo Credits: Cover © Galen Rowell/Corbis; p. 5 © Peter Oxford/Nature Picture Library;
p. 7 © Stephen Frink/Corbis; p. 9 © Eric and David Hosking/Corbis; p. 11 © Bob Krist/Corbis;
p. 13 © Peter Johnson/Corbis; p. 15 © Jim Zuckerman/Corbis; p. 17 © Wolfgang Kaehler/Corbis;
p. 19 © Bruce Davidson/Nature Picture Library; p. 21 © Martin Harvey, Gallo Images/Corbis
Contributing Editor: Jennifer Silate
Book Design: Mindy Liu

Library of Congress Cataloging-in-Publication Data

Eckart, Edana.
    African elephant / by Edana Eckart.
    v. cm.—(Animals of the world)
    Contents: The largest land animal—The trunk—The tusks.
    ISBN 0-516-24301-2 (lib. bdg.)—ISBN 0-516-27879-7 (pbk.)
    1. African elephant—Juvenile literature. [1. African elephant. 2.
Elephants.] I. Title. II. Series: Eckart, Edana.   Animals of the
world.

    QL737.P98E36 2003
    599.67'4—dc21

                                              2002154956

African elephants are very tall.

They can reach the tops of trees.

The African elephant has a long **trunk**.

It uses its trunk to smell.

African elephants also use their trunks to eat.

Elephants eat grass, leaves, and fruit.

They use their trunks to grab their food.

An African elephant uses its trunk to drink, too.

It sucks water into its trunk.

Then, the elephant **squirts** the water into its mouth.

An African elephant's front teeth are called **tusks**.

Tusks grow to be very large.

African elephants also have very large ears.

Elephants can hear
very well.

African elephants travel in groups.

A group of elephants is called a **herd**.

Many people use African elephants to do work.

African elephants are very strong and **powerful** animals.

21

New Words

African elephant (**af**-ruh-kuhn **el**-uh-fuhnt) a very big mammal with a large head, big ears, and a long nose called a trunk, that lives in Africa

herd (**hurd**) a large group of animals, such as elephants

powerful (**pou**-ur-fuhl) having the ability to do things or make things happen

squirts (**skwurts**) to send out a stream of liquid

trunk (**truhngk**) an elephant's long nose

tusks (**tuhsks**) the pair of long, curved, pointed teeth of an elephant

To Find Out More

Books
African Elephants
by Roland Smith
Lerner Publishing Group

The Elephant
by Mymi Doinet
Abbeville Press

Web Site
San Francisco Zoo: African Elephant
http://www.sfzoo.org/cgi-bin/animals.py?ID=68
Learn many interesting facts about the African elephant
on this Web site.

Index

ears, 16

herd, 18

smell, 8

squirts, 12

trunk, 8, 10, 12

tusks, 14

About the Author
Edana Eckart has written several children's books. She enjoys bike riding with her family.

Reading Consultants

Kris Flynn, Coordinator, Small School District Literacy, The San Diego County Office of Education

Shelly Forys, Certified Reading Recovery Specialist, W.J. Zahnow Elementary School, Waterloo, IL

Sue McAdams, Former President of the North Texas Reading Council of the IRA, and Early Literacy Consultant, Dallas, TX